Who Is Tony Hawk?

by Steve Korté
illustrated by Andrew Thomson

Penguin Workshop

For Bill, Glenn, and Rockwell—SK

For Rhia, Cerys, and Esme—AT

PENGUIN WORKSHOP
An imprint of Penguin Random House LLC
1745 Broadway, New York, New York 10019

First published in the United States of America by Penguin Workshop,
an imprint of Penguin Random House LLC, 2025

Copyright © 2025 by Penguin Random House LLC

Penguin Random House values and supports copyright. Copyright fuels creativity, encourages diverse voices, promotes free speech, and creates a vibrant culture. Thank you for buying an authorized edition of this book and for complying with copyright laws by not reproducing, scanning, or distributing any part of it in any form without permission. You are supporting writers and allowing Penguin Random House to continue to publish books for every reader. Please note that no part of this book may be used or reproduced in any manner for the purpose of training artificial intelligence technologies or systems.

PENGUIN is a registered trademark and PENGUIN WORKSHOP is a trademark
of Penguin Books Ltd. WHO HQ & Design is a registered trademark
of Penguin Random House LLC.

Visit us online at penguinrandomhouse.com.

Library of Congress Cataloging-in-Publication Data is available.

Printed in the United States of America

ISBN 9780593751800 (paperback)   10 9 8 7 6 5 4 3 2 1 CJKW
ISBN 9780593751817 (library binding)   10 9 8 7 6 5 4 3 2 1 CJKW

Contents

Who Is Tony Hawk? 1
Full of Energy 6
A History of Skateboarding 13
More than a Hobby 24
Going Professional 40
A Quick Retirement 56
Troubling Times 63
Extreme Games 68
Landing a 900 78
Branching Out 85
Still Skating 97
Timelines 106
Bibliography 108

Who Is Tony Hawk?

On June 27, 1999, Tony Hawk was standing at the top of a tall ramp in San Francisco, California. A cold wind blew around him as he stared down into the U-shaped vert (short for vertical) ramp. The ramp had been specially designed for skateboarders, allowing them to zoom down and then up each side, building up speed in order to perform dazzling skateboarding tricks in the air.

Tony and Andy Macdonald

Tony was participating in the Summer 1999 X Games competition. The ESPN sports channel was going to broadcast the show, and they had invited Tony and four other top vert skaters—Colin McKay, Andy Macdonald, Bucky Lasek, and Bob Burnquist—to skate in a "best trick" competition.

The crowd in the stands was excited. Each skater performed well. Andy Macdonald and

Colin McKay did a series of impressive tricks, and it looked like they might win the competition. Then Bucky Lasek did some amazing tricks. Tony Hawk had only minutes left to perform and try to win the contest.

At the time, Tony Hawk was the most famous skateboarder in the world. He was thirty-one years old and had won countless skateboarding competitions. He had invented more than one hundred skateboard tricks that other skaters had tried—and often failed—to duplicate. But there was one trick that Tony had not yet mastered. It was called "the 900," and it meant flying up into the air on a skateboard and completing an incredible two and a half flips before landing. No skater had ever been known to successfully perform the 900. Tony had injured himself several times in the past trying to do the trick. He had his doubts that it was even possible to land one.

As Tony stood high above the ground, getting ready to skate down the ramp, the crowd in the stadium started chanting, "Tony! Tony! Tony!"

When Tony launched himself off the top of the ramp, his mind was made up. He decided that he was going to be the first person ever to perform and land a perfect 900!

Not only did Tony Hawk complete the difficult and dazzling 900 that day, but he continued to skate and to influence generations of other skaters. During an amazing career that has lasted for decades, Tony became a hero to millions of kids who were learning how to skate. It wasn't always easy. Over the years, Tony had lots of ups and downs, both in his life and on his boards. But with hard work, determination, and a little luck, Tony Hawk became the first superstar of skateboarding.

CHAPTER 1
Full of Energy

Anthony "Tony" Hawk was born on May 12, 1968, in San Diego, California. His parents, Frank and Nancy, were both in their early forties when Tony was born. Tony was the youngest of four children. His two sisters, Pat and Lenore, were already adults living away from home. His brother, Steve, was twelve years old when Tony arrived.

"I was basically an only child," Tony later said. "My parents were old enough to be my grandparents."

As a child, Tony was full of energy. In fact, most people thought he had *too* much energy. He later described himself as an "absolute nightmare" in the way he treated his parents. But his parents made it very clear that they loved him, even though he wasn't always the best-behaved son.

"I'm not proud of my attitude as a child," Tony said. "Now, I understand that part of my problem was my diet. My parents usually let me eat what I wanted. They had little choice—I would throw a temper tantrum if I didn't get it. I ate sugar-coated cereals and ice cream every day. I drank more Coke than water. All the sugar and caffeine cranked me up into a frenzy, and once it mixed with my overachieving determination, I could barely control myself."

Tony was also very hard on himself and had a strong fear of failing at his many after-school activities, including violin lessons, swimming, baseball, and basketball. He felt that he was disappointing others if he didn't perform well at everything he tried.

"I had an overactive sense of determination, which exploded whenever I was involved in anything competitive," Tony recalled. "If I thought I was losing at checkers, I'd flip the board up, spraying checkers all over the room. If somebody had something I wanted, such as a Frisbee, I'd have to have it. If there were three or four people with Frisbees, it wasn't enough that they shared one with me—I had to have them all! I was a brat of Godzilla proportions."

Tony got high grades at school, and when he was in the second grade, his parents took him to a psychologist, a person who analyzes behavior. Tests showed that Tony was very intelligent. That put him in the "gifted" category.

Tony said, "The person who administered

the test explained that the cause of my frustration was that my brain was constantly telling my body to do things it couldn't physically do." Tony was still so young that he didn't know how to properly express his irritation and anger. "Because of this, I burned myself out trying to accomplish my goals and was usually disappointed with myself when I didn't meet them. So I took out my frustration on my family."

One day when Tony was nine years old, his brother, Steve, was rummaging around in the garage and found his old, dusty skateboard. It was a blue fiberglass (a type of plastic) board made by the Bahne company. Steve handed it to Tony and suggested that he give it a try. Tony stepped into an alley behind their house and hopped on the board. He promptly slammed into a fence at the end of the alley. Steve patiently taught Tony how to stop and how to turn around on the board.

"I had a good time skating that day," Tony remembered, "but to me it was the same as playing miniature golf or throwing a Frisbee around—fun, but nothing I craved doing nonstop."

Tony and Steve

Around this same time, on the other side of the country, a thirteen-year-old boy in Florida named Alan "Ollie" Gelfand was inventing a new skateboarding move. Without using his hands, Alan was able to launch his skateboard into the air by stomping on the back of the board to get it nearly vertical. He then moved his front foot forward to level out the skateboard at the peak of the jump. The trick, created in 1978, became known as the "ollie."

By the time that Alan had invented the ollie, Tony Hawk decided that skateboarding *was* kind of fun after all. He began skating a few times a week.

Alan "Ollie" Gelfand

CHAPTER 2
A History of Skateboarding

Ever since the invention of the wheel, people have experimented with different ways of using wheels to travel. Both kids and adults have long tried to perfect the idea of having wheels under their feet.

Roller skates—shoes with wheels at the bottom—first appeared in the late 1700s. An inventor from Belgium named John Joseph Merlin is credited with creating the first roller skate in 1760 when he attached two metal wheels each to a pair

John Joseph Merlin

of boots. One evening, Merlin demonstrated his new invention at a fancy dinner party and crashed into a large mirror. The accident almost killed him, and has gone down in history as perhaps the first fall in the history of skating.

Over the centuries, roller skates evolved into shoes with wheels attached to them—similar in design to ice skates—but the problem with those kind of skates (roller and ice) was that people, especially children, would outgrow the shoes. Eventually, expandable metal clamp-on roller skates were developed that could be attached to a regular pair of shoes.

Roller skates definitely played a role in the creation of the skateboard, but there is another item that was perhaps an even bigger influence. The modern skateboard is a direct descendent of the Hawaiian *papa he'e nalu*, which we now call a surfboard.

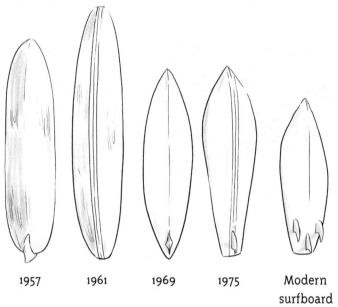

1957   1961   1969   1975   Modern surfboard

During the 1930s, surfing became popular around the world, especially in Hawaii and California. When the sea was calm, the surfers

Skateboarding in the early 1960s

wanted another way to re-create the thrill of riding the big waves. The solution was to build a scaled-down version of a surfboard that they could ride on land. Someone came up with the bright idea of taking the wheels from a roller skate and attaching them to a small plank of surfboard-shaped wood. The skateboard was born!

The design of a skateboard is pretty simple. It's just a narrow board with four wheels attached to its underside. The top part, where a rider puts their feet, is called the deck. There are metal pieces below the deck called trucks, which hold the wheels in place.

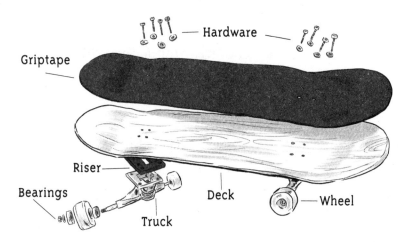

In 1958, Roller Derby, a toy manufacturer, released the first mass-produced skateboard, the Little Red. It had steel wheels attached to each end of a plywood board. Skateboarding grew in popularity, starting in California and soon spreading to the rest of the country. Kids were skateboarding on sidewalks, streets, and alleys.

Little Red skateboard by Roller Derby

Over the next ten years, manufacturers improved the design of skateboards, replacing the steel wheels with clay ones that gave riders greater control on pavement.

During the 1960s, some adults viewed skateboarding with suspicion. Watching a skateboarder zoom by on a sidewalk was frightening to some people. Skateboarders sometimes caused serious injuries to themselves and others. Some communities even made skateboarding illegal!

Skateboarding had already caught kids' imaginations, though, and its popularity was only growing.

Street Skating vs. Vert Skating

The two most common types of skateboarding are street skating and vert skating. Both are very popular.

Street skateboarding, which is sometimes called freestyle skating, is done on roads, benches, curbs, plazas, and other public places. All you need is a skateboard and a flat surface to ride on.

Vert (short for vertical) skateboarding began when skaters rode their boards up and down the curved walls of empty swimming pools. Eventually, people started building bowls—structures that were similar to the high, curved walls of some pools. Other popular structures for vert skating are ramps and the halfpipe, a half circle that looks like a large pipe cut in half.

In 1972, a company called Cadillac Wheels introduced new skateboard wheels that were made of a material called urethane. These new wheels gripped the surface of sidewalks better than clay wheels and created a smoother ride. The boards themselves were also redesigned over the years. Instead of a flat piece of wood, manufacturers made boards out of fiberglass or plastic and added a raised front or a lip in the back. These improvements allowed the riders to create new skating tricks.

Skateboard parks that were filled with ramps and cement bowls soon appeared all across the United States. Skateboard manufacturers began to sponsor skating contests at the parks.

By the late 1970s, when Tony Hawk started experimenting with his brother's dusty board, skateboarding had become a very big business.

CHAPTER 3
More than a Hobby

In 1978, Tony was in the fourth grade, and skateboarding had become his favorite activity.

He hopped on a board whenever he could, riding around the neighborhood with friends. Then Tony discovered Oasis, a skating park in San Diego that was around twenty minutes away from his home. And it was love at first sight.

"The place always seemed to be packed," Tony recalled. "It was a few acres of gray concrete,

Oasis Skatepark

polka-dotted with off-white pools. There were two big pools; a snake run, which is a long, twisted series of hips and banks that resembles a snake; a reservoir, a halfpipe with no flatbottom; and a flat beginner's area.

"When I saw people flying all around—literally flying in and out of bowls—that is when I knew I wanted to do it," he said. "I wanted to figure out how I could get there and how I could fly."

There was just one problem. Tony had always been a skinny kid, and nearly all the other skaters in the park were bigger and stronger than Tony. So Tony had to work extra hard to propel himself up a wall and fly through the air on his board.

Skateboard Slang

Over time, skateboarders have developed their own special language. These are some of the most popular skateboarding terms:

Air: Riding up the side of a ramp and launching into the air

Bail: Stepping or jumping off your board when something goes wrong

Burly: Any high-risk trick that could lead to serious injuries if not completed successfully

Fakie: Riding your skateboard backward

Land: To successfully complete a trick

Sick: A really good rider or trick

Snake: A skater who doesn't wait their turn at a skate park

Stick: To land a trick properly

Stoked: Getting excited

Thrasher: An enthusiastic skater

Varial: Rotating the board with your foot while flying through the air

Varial flip

Many times he would experience a slam, which was how skaters described an unexpected fall to the ground or collision against a wall. Although Tony always wore a helmet, elbow pads, and knee pads, he admitted that he became a "walking scab" from all his slams.

Skateboarding legend Stacy Peralta witnessed some of Tony's early skating attempts and remembered, "Tony did not display any physical talent. But the one thing that he did have is, you could see . . . this intense determination. You could see in there, there was a mind going, 'Do this! Do this!'"

Another famous skateboarder named Mike McGill said, "The first time I saw Tony, I was like,

Mike McGill

'Look at this little kid.' He was probably, I don't know, sixty pounds wet, maybe."

Tony started skating nonstop at Oasis. Much to the surprise of both Tony and his parents, he experienced a strange side effect.

"I became nicer," said Tony. "I remember thinking one day, 'I'm tired of being a jerk to my parents.' Skating made me focus on improving myself rather than dwelling on my immature frustrations."

Stacy Peralta (1957–)

Stacy Peralta was born in Venice, California, where skateboarding was—and still is—hugely popular. He started skating when he was young, and by the age of fifteen had become one of the top members of the Zephyr Competition Team, also known as the Z-Boys. After suffering several wrist injuries when he was in his early twenties, he retired from skating and formed a successful skateboard company with George Powell called Powell-Peralta. He then recruited the best skaters to join the company's newly-formed team of skaters called the Bones Brigade.

During the 1980s, Stacy directed a series of popular skateboard videos, including *The Search for Animal Chin*. He also worked as an actor and director in several feature films, including *Real Genius* and *Gleaming the Cube*. In 2001, he cowrote the acclaimed documentary film *Dogtown and Z-Boys*. Four years later, he wrote the screenplay for the movie *Lords of Dogtown*.

"He just needed focus, and so when he started focusing and skateboarding," said his sister Pat, "he changed."

Tony's brother, Steve, also noticed that Tony seemed to be more mature and even more generous.

Tony's parents fully approved of his new interest and took him to Oasis almost every day. He was a big fan of the daredevil motorcyclist Evel Knievel, and soon Tony started experimenting with skateboard tricks. It wasn't easy, though.

Evel Knievel

"I was too light to grab airs early," he said, referring to a skateboarder's ability to fly up off the ramp or bowl and soar through the air. "I had to work extra hard to get enough speed to propel myself out of the bowl, and if I bent down to grab [my board], I would lose my momentum. The only way I could figure out how to do it was to pop an ollie, and once I was in the air, grab my board. I ollied into my airs."

At the time, no other skater was using an ollie to get into the air, and Tony admitted that it looked weird.

"I was embarrassed about not being able to skate like everybody else—other skaters made fun of me and called me a 'circus skater,'" said Tony. "Little did I know that in ten years, they and every skater would be doing airs using my technique.

"When I decided to learn a trick, nothing could get in my way," Tony remembered.

Tony's father, Frank, supported Tony's hobby so much that in 1980, he formed the California Amateur Skateboard League (CASL), which organized competitions for skateboarders. Soon, Tony started winning every CASL competition. Then he got his first sponsor, a skateboard company called Dogtown. Being sponsored wasn't that big a deal to Tony. But having a sponsor meant that he didn't have to pay for his equipment.

Every now and then, Dogtown sent him a free board.

Tony started to wonder if he could become a professional skateboarder like one of his favorite skaters, Rodney Mullen. Rodney was a member of the skateboarding team called the Bones Brigade, which had been founded by Stacy Peralta. The Bones Brigade traveled all across the country, competing for cash prizes in professional skating contests. Also, if Tony "went pro," he

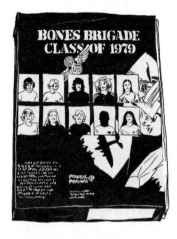

could perhaps earn money by endorsing skateboard products.

"In the early eighties, [the Bones Brigade] was the team to be on," Tony said. "One time I was at the skate park, and the Bones Brigade showed up. And you just knew it immediately. There was a hush in the skate park. Everyone on the team were considered some of the best skaters. Stacy was walking in with these guys, and they all had these, like cool-colored helmets and their Bones Brigade shirts. And I was just like, 'This is the future.'"

Tony had a lot of confidence in himself, but he wasn't sure if he was big enough—or skilled enough—to skate with a team like the Bones Brigade.

Rodney Mullen (1966–)

Rodney Mullen was born in Gainesville, Florida, and started skating at the age of ten in his family garage. After only a year, he started winning skateboard competitions. In the 1980s, Rodney won  thirty-four out of thirty-five freestyle skating contests. He skated as a member of the Bones Brigade team, and appeared in several skating video games.

Rodney is often called the "Godfather of modern street skating" and has been credited with inventing many popular street skating tricks, including the street ollie, kick-flip, heel-flip, 360-flip, impossible, and many more.

CHAPTER 4
Going Professional

As Tony continued to skate in the CASL competitions, he soon mastered the tricks performed by older, more experienced skaters. Still, he wasn't completely satisfied. He knew that the key to improving his skating skills was to get creative and to invent some new tricks of his own.

Sometimes, Tony would add a flip to a trick, or twist his body in an unusual way. One of his new tricks included the ollie 540, in which he performed an ollie and then spun around one and a half times without holding on to his board. Other new tricks included the 360 kick-flip mute grab, the popshuvit nosegrind, and the varial 540. Tony even came up with the names for his new tricks.

During one CASL contest, Stacy Peralta approached Tony and told him that he liked Tony's skating.

"I was so happy about being noticed and complimented by a legend like Stacy that I can't remember the rest of the contest at all," Tony said.

At the end of 1980, after the skateboard company Dogtown went out of business, Stacy decided to not only sponsor Tony, but also invite him to join the Bones Brigade. At twelve years old, Tony became the team's youngest member.

He was still competing in amateur contests, but he felt the pressure to skate even better to impress his famous teammates. It wasn't easy.

"If you think I'm skinny now, you should have seen me in the seventh grade when I was growing," Tony remembered years later. "Birds could have used me for nesting material. Muscle tone was something I'd only read about. I was twelve years old, barely over four feet tall, and weighed in at a freakish eighty pounds (and that was after a big meal). I was a walking noodle."

In 1982, just a few months after Tony's fourteenth birthday, he decided to become a professional skateboarder. At the time, going pro didn't seem like that big a deal to Tony. When he told his parents that he had turned professional, the Hawks simply said, "That's nice."

Back then, professional skateboarding was not the big business it is today. In the early 1980s, contest winnings for professional skateboarders were usually quite low—$150 for first place, $100 for second, and $50 for third. And skateboard contests didn't attract big crowds.

"In my first contest, I placed third," Tony said. "There were at least eighteen people in the stands watching my professional debut. I didn't win any money."

Tony's dad had successfully gotten the CASL up and running, and now he decided to turn his attention to professional skateboarding. In 1983, Frank Hawk started the National

Skateboard Association (NSA). That created some problems for the youngest member of the Bones Brigade.

"Skaters and people involved in the business appreciated what my dad was doing, but I felt the pressure right away," Tony said. "I was a relatively new pro, and my dad was running the official contest series. People started whispering that contests might be fixed in my favor."

However, Tony didn't need any help from his dad to win contests. In 1983, Tony was declared the first NSA world vert champion. He went on to win many more NSA competitions. He also created dozens of new tricks. By time he turned sixteen, Tony had landed four more sponsors in addition to Powell-Peralta: Tracker, Sundek, SIO, and Vans.

Tony became a skateboarding superstar. It was

in his mid-teens that he picked up the nickname "Birdman." It refers to his last name and also to his ability to fly through the air on his skateboard. Tony traveled around the world, winning one competition after another. At a skate park in Del Mar, California, he became the first known skater to launch his board out of a pool using just the force of his body. Before that, a skater would have to go up and down the sides of a bowl over and over to build up enough speed to soar through the air. With that one move, Tony revolutionized the art of vert skating.

Vans

Unlike most traditional sports—such as baseball, basketball, and football—there are no official skateboarding uniforms. When it comes to skateboarding footwear, though, there is one clear favorite. That's the Vans line of skateboard shoes.

The brand made its debut in 1966 as the Van Doren Rubber Company. They manufactured shoes with thick rubber soles and sold them in their own store in Southern California for as little as $2.49. The shoes quickly became popular with skaters, and by the mid-1970s, Vans was the most successful manufacturer of skateboard shoes. In 1976, the company started advertising their shoes using the motto "Off the Wall," which was a phrase that skaters used to describe doing tricks in empty swimming pools. One year later, Vans introduced its Old Skool skateboard shoes, also known as #36. With its bold stripe running along the side, the shoe was hugely successful, and decades later is still one of the most popular Vans models worldwide.

Over the years, the company has shown its commitment to skateboarding by sponsoring skating competitions and building skate parks.

"He grew taller than all of us," said Mike McGill. "His tricks got bigger, and his airs got higher. He was coming up with a fantastic run, and then all of a sudden, he'd one-up himself."

"At every contest there'd be like three new tricks," professional skateboarder Christian Hosoi recalled. "He's spinning, he's varialing, he's doing finger flips [flipping the board with your hand after making the jump]. Here I am just trying to go higher, farther, faster, 'cause I have to keep up with Tony."

Christian Hosoi

When he was fourteen, Tony was rated the best skateboarder in the world! He was about to become even more famous, thanks to Stacy.

In 1984, Stacy's company, Powell-Peralta, produced a skateboard video called *The Bones Brigade Video Show*. The entire team skated in the video, and the front cover of the video package had a  big picture of Tony flying through the air on his board. The plan was that skateboard shops would play the video in their stores and hopefully sell more boards and accessories. But kids all across the country started buying the video to watch at home. They could play and replay it over and over. And they could hit "pause" and freeze on an image, trying to figure out just how Tony Hawk did his tricks.

Tony's Top Tricks

It is estimated that Tony has created more than a hundred skateboard tricks. Here are three of his most impressive ones:

1. Kick-flip McTwist: This difficult trick combines a kick-flip (moving your foot so that your board spins 360 degrees) with a McTwist (a front flip with a 540-degree spin). This all happens while the skater is flying through the air. During this trick, the board spins 360 degrees and the skater spins 540 degrees (a full spin-and-a-half) at the same time.

2. 720: To perform this trick, a rider grabs their board and spins two full rotations while flying through the air. You need a lot of speed and height off the ramp to pull off this trick.

3. 720 ollie: The skater comes up backward, spins around twice on a vertical axis without grabbing the board, and then lands. This is the trick that had challenged Tony the most. At the age of fifty-two, he finally landed it.

720 ollie

The year 1986 was big for Tony. The first official Tony Hawk skateboard was released by the Powell-Peralta company, which soon started selling as many as twenty thousand of the boards a month. Tony earned a dollar for each board sold. That same year, Tony made his first big screen appearance as an extra in the movie *Thrashin'*. He went on a nationwide tour with the Bones Brigade. And just before he graduated from high school, Tony took the money that he had earned from skateboarding and bought his first house. He was just seventeen years old.

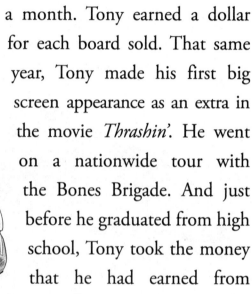

Everything seemed to be going great, but Tony started to feel burned out by the nonstop touring and competing against other skaters. He felt sad if he didn't win first place in a contest.

"I had won every vert world championship title since the start of the NSA," he said. "But it was too much pressure for me. Even though I often won, I had to outperform myself, not other competitors. I was miserable and started to get depressed. I spoke to Stacy about quitting contests. To my surprise, he supported me. Both of us were unsure of what lay ahead if I stopped competing. Would I continue to make a living?"

Tony made the big decision to quit competitive skateboarding.

CHAPTER 5
A Quick Retirement

After he retired from competing, Tony bought a second home in a desert town in California and built a huge vert ramp in his backyard.

He started having fun skating again. It reminded him of his skating days at Oasis. After just three months of retirement, Tony announced that he was ready to compete again. The joy of skating had returned to him.

"I found my way back to it with a different attitude," Tony said. "I was skating for fun, and if people thought I lost when I got second place,

it didn't bother me anymore. I had a totally different approach to what I was doing."

Tony went back on the road with the Bones Brigade. He filmed two small skating roles in the movies *Gleaming the Cube* and *Police Academy 4*.

In the late 1980s, Tony became an even bigger star. He and his teammates were earning more money than he could spend.

"It seemed like money was just raining down, and some of the guys got carried away," Tony remembered. "They were spending crazy. At one point [Powell-Peralta] sent us credit cards. We had no idea how credit cards worked, so we just thought that we could spend money and that we wouldn't get the bill. We were buying cameras, video games. I think I bought a pinball machine."

Everything was going great for Tony. A skateboard that he designed became a top seller. Skateboarding became more popular than ever, especially as kids developed their street skating skills. Now thousands of fans showed up for each Bones Brigade show.

In 1989, the team toured the United States for a month. Every demonstration they did brought out thousands of fans. After that, the Bones Brigade toured Europe and Australia, where they attracted huge crowds. In Sydney, Australia, a vert ramp was built in the middle of the city, and people watched the competition from their rooftops because there was no more room on the ground for spectators.

Tony married his high-school sweetheart, Cindy Dunbar, in 1990. He was almost twenty-two. Cindy was twenty-four.

Their son, Riley, was born in 1992, and it wasn't long before Riley showed an interest in skateboarding, too.

But soon after, the sport of skateboarding took a huge downturn in popularity.

CHAPTER 6
Troubling Times

After attracting a huge number of fans in the 1980s—partly due to Tony Hawk—the sport of skateboarding started to fall from favor in the early 1990s. Skateboard sales declined, and many skate parks closed. There were fewer contests

and smaller audiences at the Bones Brigade shows. Soon, professional skate contests almost disappeared.

"The early nineties were the dark years," said Mike McGill. "It was tough. Vertical skateboarding was dead."

Tony still believed in skateboarding, though. In 1992, he made the bold decision to form his own skateboard company called Birdhouse.

Birdhouse

The first years of the company were rough. Tony was forced to sell one of his houses, and he started taking every odd job he could to earn money. But he continued to skate.

"I never considered quitting skating as an option," said Tony. "I loved skating my backyard ramp, but I had no money to fix it. I had to dodge holes that were rotting into it."

In 1993, Tony organized a Birdhouse Summer Tour and loaded five skaters into his cramped minivan. They drove around the country for a month, but ended up losing thousands of dollars on the tour.

Tony and Cindy divorced in 1994, but they remained friends and agreed to make their son, Riley, their top priority. Just about the only bright spot that year was when Tony met and fell in love with a woman named Erin Lee.

Tony and Erin Lee

"By 1995 I was convinced that my involvement in the skateboarding industry was coming to an end," said Tony. "I wasn't sure if Birdhouse could last another year without a big jump in sales. But as much of a bummer as 1994 was (except for meeting Erin), the following year was like riding an out-of-control roller coaster."

That next year was about to bring some of the highest highs and lowest lows of Tony's life.

CHAPTER 7
Extreme Games

Things started looking up for Tony in 1995. Sales of Birdhouse skateboards slowly increased as street skating once again became popular. A few companies started building skate parks again so kids could explore vert skating. Tony's life was happy with Erin. His three-year-old son, Riley, was even able to do an ollie!

Tony kept busy touring, his company Birdhouse began making money, and Tony and Erin made plans to get married.

Early in 1995, the ESPN channel had announced that they would showcase an Olympics-style sporting event called the Extreme Games. Unlike the Olympics, though, it would feature twenty-seven alternative (less traditional) sports,

including motocross, rock climbing, rollerblading, and skateboarding. Tony skated in the first Extreme Games and won first place in vert skating and second place in street skating.

"When the camera filmed me, I looked into it and said, 'Hi, Dad.' I knew he'd get a kick out of that, because nobody bragged about me as much as my dad. I was surprised at how many people recognized me after the contest aired on TV, but, more important, I was excited that skating had been seen by millions of people around the world."

In July, Frank Hawk passed away from lung cancer. Hundreds of people attended his funeral, including the entire skateboarding community.

"People who had been involved in skating over the previous twenty years came over and exchanged affectionate stories about my dad grumbling and complaining around skate contests, but loving it at the same time," said Tony. "Skaters who were troublemakers told me that my dad's influence helped change their lives for the better. I knew that would have pleased my dad and meant more to him than anything else he'd done for skating."

That same year, Tony slammed hard at a

contest in Seal Beach, California, and sprained his ankle. He couldn't take the time to let it heal because a Birdhouse tour was about to start. Two weeks later during the tour, he sprained his other ankle just as badly. The pain was so terrible that Tony actually considered retiring again.

The Extreme Games was a big success, and in 1996, ESPN changed its name to the X Games. Tony participated in each new edition of the X Games, and a Birdhouse tour attracted big crowds again. Tony and Erin were married that same year.

The following year, Tony decided it was time to finally master a trick called the 900. This trick is done by skating down a ramp, soaring up the other side and launching into the air, then completing two and a half revolutions—or 900 degrees—while spinning through the air. No skater had ever been able to pull it off. Tony himself had once broken a rib trying to do a 900! He tried to perform 900s on the X Games, but he just couldn't land one.

In 1998, he and Stacy worked on a skating video called *The End*. Tony decided to call it *The End* because he was about to turn thirty, and he figured that his best skateboarding days might soon be behind him. No professional skater had been successfully competitive past that age.

For *The End*, Tony had a ramp with a giant loop built in a Mexican bullring. He had tried to skate a loop once before for a TV commercial, but he had lost control when he exited and wiped out on his back.

"Landing the loop and a 900 were two of my

main goals for the video," said Tony.

Tony managed to land the loop for the video—even though he was suffering from a back injury—but no matter how hard he tried, he just couldn't perform a 900.

Fans didn't seem to mind, though. *The End*

was a huge success. And best of all for Tony, shortly after the video was released, his second son, Spencer, was born.

CHAPTER 8
Landing a 900

In 1999, Tony once again made the decision to stop skating in contests.

"It wasn't due to any crushing pressures that I felt," he explained. "It was the sense that I was satisfied with what I had accomplished. After fifteen years of pro contests, I wanted to return to the days when I just skated with my friends."

But Tony had one big professional goal left: to nail the 900.

"I had never gotten so close to a trick and given up on it," Tony said. "Never. Someone's got to do this. Someone's got to break through this boundary."

"When he's going after a trick, you can watch him get closer and closer, 'cause he's making little adjustments in his head," observed fellow skater Sean Mortimer. "When he knows he's getting close, he does not give up on a trick unless his body breaks. He'll just throw himself and slam, slam, slam, slam. The 900 was a little different, 'cause that really trashes your body super quick."

Tarzan and Tony

In 1999, the Walt Disney studio released the animated movie *Tarzan.* After the movie came out, one of its artists told Tony that some of his skating moves in *The End* had inspired the animators when they were drawing Tarzan's movements swinging through the trees. Tony's son Riley was especially impressed with this news.

"My fame from skating meant nothing to him," Tony said of his son, "but being involved in a Disney movie—now I was cool."

Tony and Riley even filmed a commercial for the movie's home video release.

On June 27, 1999, Tony skated in the fifth edition of the X Games. One of the categories for skateboarders was best trick. Tony and four other top vert skaters—Colin McKay, Andy Macdonald, Bucky Lasek, and Bob Burnquist—had a total of twenty minutes to perform. Tony landed a varial 720 during the first part of his competition. With fifteen minutes left to go, Tony walked back up the ramp, thinking of what trick to attempt next. He decided to go for a 900.

"I had been attempting 900s for more than ten years," he said. "I remembered the last time I'd thought I was close to landing one. I ended up slamming into the ramp, fracturing a rib. Another time before that I got lost in the middle of the spin, landed on top of the ramp, bounced off the flatbottom. There were parts of the trick, such as how to control the spin and adjust my weight for the landing, that I just didn't know how to do. Once I would solve one problem, another would present itself. I had my doubts that it was even possible to land one."

Tony flew down the ramp and up the other side and then flipped through the air. There were gasps in the stadium as the other skaters and the fans realized that Tony was going for the 900. He crashed and slid down the ramp on his knees.

But he got back up and tried again. And again, eleven more times. The twenty-minute timer had gone off, but the cheering crowd didn't care.

Tony was given extra time by the judges, and his competitors encouraged him to keep going.

"Tony! Tony! Tony!" chanted the crowd.

And then, on his twelfth attempt, Tony became the first skateboarder to land a 900! The astonished crowd went wild.

"My fist shot up automatically, and I yelled as loud as I could," Tony remembered. "All the skaters ran onto the ramp and tackled me before picking me up and carrying me around. It was the happiest moment of my skate career."

After this amazing accomplishment, Tony realized that he was ready to leave the world of skateboarding competitions. At the end of the year, he officially retired from competitions.

CHAPTER 9
Branching Out

After he retired in 1999, Tony thought that his life would get less hectic. But the opposite happened. He continued to compete in the X Games until 2003. And he stayed busier than ever, both in his personal life and his skating career. Back in 1986, Atari had released an arcade game called *720°*, which was named after a trick invented by Tony. In the 1990s, as the technology improved, home video games became even more popular.

In 1999, Activision launched a home video game titled *Tony Hawk's Pro Skater*. It allowed video

game players to skate alongside Tony, compete with him, and learn from him. The game became the best-selling PlayStation game in the world in 2000! Since then, there have been eighteen successful follow-up releases, and over eighty versions of the games across different gaming platforms, including mobile and online versions.

"When the fourth game was released, the first three were still in the top ten of sales," Tony recalled. "And Activision called a meeting with me. I went and met one of the guys I worked with. He explained to me what was happening. He's like, 'Well, this is in the top sales, and now it's a best hit.' I go, 'What does that mean?' He goes, 'This is what it means,' and he hands me a check for $4.5 million. And I was like, 'Oh, my God.'

And then two years later, they gave me an advance of $20 million."

Tony took a job as an ESPN commentator and then created a TV show for ESPN called *Tony Hawk's Gigantic Skatepark Tour*. That got Tony thinking about the possibility of creating sports tour shows in arenas around the world. He wanted to come up with an alternative to overly regulated skating competitions.

"At its core, [skating] is about innovation and improvisations," said Tony. "It's about ignoring rules. I figured there must be a way for talented action-sports athletes to headline events without competing against one another. What if we built a portable ramp and practiced routines in advance?

Mix in some BMX riders, maybe turn up the juice with a motocross jump. Invite a good band. Call it something catchy, choreograph a whole show, take it on the road."

Tony and his friends considered a few different titles for the arena show, including Heavy Air High Boy and Speed Launch Gnarly Man. They finally settled on Boom Boom HuckJam, and in 2002, the tour was launched in Las Vegas, Nevada.

It was not easy to produce. The show needed eight tour buses to carry the sixty-member crew and fourteen semitrucks to haul the equipment, which included a giant portable ramp system. At each stop, a hundred more laborers had to be hired to install and then dismantle the set.

The show was a huge hit. It even led to a reality TV show called *Tony Hawk's HuckJam Diaries* and a tie-in series of McDonald's Happy Meal toys.

"Suddenly, we were rock stars again, but on a completely different level," said Tony. "Performing in arenas, selling out night after night. We were way bigger than a rock tour. We filled the entire arena floor with ramps and lights, pyrotechnics."

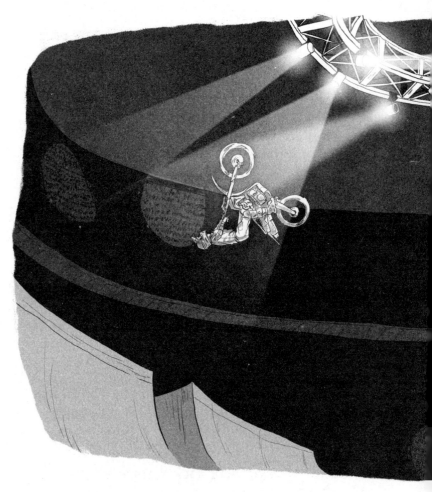

"It was high-pressure skateboarding," said skater Andy Macdonald, who joined the tour. "It was like, you have to make this trick, or a motorcycle could land on you."

Skateboarding became more popular than ever, and Tony Hawk became a mega-celebrity known around the world.

"I wish my dad had been able to see the

recognition and appreciation that skateboarding got after '99 and 2000," said Tony. "Even in his wildest dreams, he thought that skateboard contests would be bigger, but he would have never imagined that it blew up the way it did."

In 2001, Erin and Tony had another son, named Keegan, and Tony created the charitable Tony Hawk Foundation to call attention to the lack of safe and legal skate parks in America.

At the time, there were approximately twelve million skateboarders in the United States, but only about two thousand skate parks. Many poor communities couldn't afford to build skate parks. Other places were worried about lawsuits from skating accidents.

"But here's the thing," said Tony about the need for skate parks. "Kids are going to skate whether or not civic leaders create a place for them to do it. So they end up skating in spots that city officials or school administrators or local business owners have deemed off-limits. That means youngsters who'd never been in serious trouble suddenly find themselves getting ticketed or arrested or suspended—simply because they want to pursue a sport that they're passionate about. And once a kid gets on the wrong side of the law, for whatever reason, his world can speed downhill."

The first step Tony took toward the goal

of creating skate parks was to write a check for $50,000 to the foundation.

After that, Tony skated in *Jackass: The Movie*. He appeared on many television shows, including *Sesame Street*, the Nickelodeon show *Yo Gabba Gabba!*, and *CSI: Miami*. He even got to play himself on an episode of *The Simpsons* called "Barting Over."

Tony and Erin divorced in 2004. Two years later he married Lhotse Merriam, and they welcomed a daughter, Kadence Clover Hawk.

Andre Agassi and Tony Hawk for Athletes for Hope

In 2007, Tony joined forces with several other athletes, including Andre Agassi, Muhammad Ali, Jeff Gordon, and Jackie Joyner-Kersee, to form the charity Athletes for Hope, an organization that aims to inspire all people to volunteer and support their communities.

In 2011, Tony launched his online YouTube RIDE Channel. One of the shows on the channel was *Hand in Hand*, featuring musicians and artists who had been inspired by skateboarding. Another show was *Tony's Strange Life*, in which he performed in comedy skits and interviewed a wide variety of people, not just skateboarders.

Tony interviewing Frank Black of the band Pixies

Tony also consulted with a company that developed the first skateboard emoji.

That same year, at the age of forty-three, Tony posted a video on Twitter showing him successfully pulling off another 900!

CHAPTER 10
Still Skating

Tony's marriage to Lhotse ended after five years. He married Cathy Goodman in 2015, and they have been together ever since. That same year, he performed as a stunt double for Will Ferrell during a skateboarding sequence in the movie *Daddy's Home*. Tony was injured while filming that scene and required ten stitches in his leg.

Tony Hawk and Will Ferrell behind the scenes of *Daddy's Home*

He performed what he said was his final 900 on June 27, 2016, at the age of forty-eight. But that didn't mean that Tony was slowing down.

In 2022, HBO released a documentary film about him entitled *Tony Hawk: Until the Wheels Fall Off*. The film featured never-before-seen footage and interviews with Tony and his family.

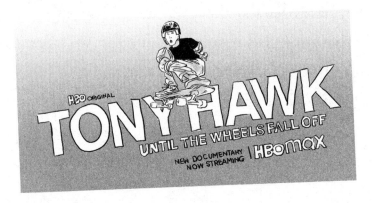

Many of Tony's favorite skaters also made appearances, including Stacy Peralta, Rodney Mullen, Mike McGill, Lance Mountain, Steve Caballero, Neil Blender, Andy Macdonald, Duane Peters, Sean Mortimer, and Christian Hosoi.

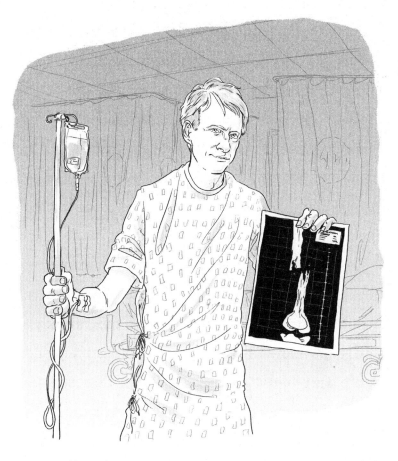

Sadly, that same year, Tony broke his femur (his thigh bone) when he messed up the landing on a McTwist, a 540-degree aerial rotation. It was a trick he had performed many times. But injuries have never slowed him down for long.

"The reason he's been hurt more than most people is because he's attempting so many more things that they would never attempt," said Stacy Peralta. "He's going to take some hits."

Fellow skater Christian Hosoi added, "You know one thing for sure about Tony is that he can take a slam. So it's rare to find people who like to get back up and try it again."

In May 2023, Tony and his foundation were able to reopen Brooklyn Banks. This was a famous skateboarding plaza under the Brooklyn Bridge in New York City that seemed beyond repair and had closed. "The idea that we are helping to revitalize it, and to reopen it, is something that I feel very lucky to be a part of," he said. Also, Tony added with a smile, it would give him a chance to skate Brooklyn Banks himself for the first time.

Later that year, Diné Skate Garden, a new skate park located in Navajo Nation in New

Mexico, was created by local organizers with assistance from Tony's foundation.

Brooklyn Banks

Tony's First Skateboard

In 1977, when he was nine years old, Tony Hawk rode a skateboard for the first time, borrowing a board that belonged to his brother, Steve. Thirty-six years later, that same skateboard found a new home when Tony donated it to the Smithsonian's National Museum of American History in Washington, DC.

Tony rode it for the last time on a mini-ramp outside the museum in 2013.

"I have ridden hundreds—if not thousands—of skateboards over the past four decades and have lost, broken, or given away most of them. Somehow this first board stayed with me, as if it knew of its importance more than I did. I never imagined that it would be considered an item of great value or significance, so I was shocked and honored when the Smithsonian offered to take it and put it on display. But I had to ask my brother first, as it was his to begin with."

"I never expected to make a career out of skateboarding," Tony said. "I think I lasted so long as a professional skater because I was always thankful for what skateboarding did for me. Skating taught me self-discipline at a young age and helped channel my frustrations and turn them into something useful. Even if I hadn't been successful at it—if I'd never made a dime—I would still be pushing around with my kids at the local skate park. I don't know anything that's as fun as skateboarding, or any activity that could have better shaped my life."

What will the future hold for Tony Hawk?

"I'm still trying to push my limits," he added. "I don't know how long this will last, but I'm not gonna quit."

Timeline of Tony Hawk's Life

1968	Anthony Hawk is born on May 12 in San Diego, California
1978	First skates at the Oasis Skatepark in San Diego
1980	Is sponsored by Dogtown
1981	Joins the Bones Brigade skate team
1984	Appears in *The Bones Brigade Video Show* skateboarding video
1986	Releases the first official Tony Hawk skateboard
	Appears in the movie *Thrashin'*
1992	Creates the Birdhouse company
1995	Skates in ESPN's Extreme Games
1999	Lands a 900 at X Games V (Five)
	Tony Hawk's Pro Skater video game is released by Activision
2001	Creates the Tony Hawk Foundation (later renamed the Skatepark Project)
2002	The Boom Boom HuckJam arena show makes its debut in Las Vegas, Nevada
2013	Donates the first skateboard he rode to the Smithsonian
2022	The documentary *Tony Hawk: Until the Wheels Fall Off* premiers on HBO
2024	Attends the Summer Olympics in Paris, France, and takes a test run on the official skateboarding course

Timeline of the World

1968	Civil rights leader Martin Luther King Jr. is assassinated
1969	Neil Armstrong becomes the first person to walk on the moon
1974	The game Dungeons & Dragons is released in the United States
1981	The cable television network MTV starts broadcasting music videos
1984	Apple releases its first Macintosh personal computer
1987	The world population reaches five billion
1989	The first episode of *The Simpsons* airs on December 17, on the FOX network
1994	Disney's *The Lion King* animated movie is released
2004	Mark Zuckerberg and a group of friends form Facebook
2016	The TikTok app launches in China
2021	A cargo ship crashes into a side of the Suez Canal in Egypt and blocks the canal's shipping lane for six days
2023	Taylor Swift Eras Tour earns more than $1 billion, and Swift is named *Time* magazine's person of the year

Bibliography

***Books for young readers**

*Braun, Eric. ***Tony Hawk***. Minneapolis: Lerner Publishing Group, 2004.

Davis, Garry, et al. ***Tony Hawk: A Life in Skateboarding***. Oceanside, CA: TransWorld SKATEboarding Magazine, 2003.

*Donovan, Sandra. ***Cool Skateboarding Facts***. Mankato, MN: Capstone Press, 2011.

Gordon, Betsy, and Jane Rogers. ***Four Wheels and a Board: The Smithsonian History of Skateboarding***. Washington, DC: Smithsonian Books, 2022.

Hawk, Tony. ***Between Boardslides and Burnout: My Notes from the Road***. New York: ReganBooks, 2002.

Hawk, Tony, with Pat Hawk. ***How Did I Get Here? The Ascent of an Unlikely CEO***. Hoboken: John Wiley & Sons, 2010.

Hawk, Tony, with Sean Mortimer. ***Hawk: Occupation: Skateboarder***. New York: ReganBooks, 2000.

Hawk, Tony, with Sean Mortimer. ***Tony Hawk Professional Skateboarder***. New York: Dey St., 2002.

*Lakin, Patricia. ***Skateboards***. New York: Aladdin, 2017.

*Stout, Glenn. ***On the Halfpipe with . . . Tony Hawk***. Boston: Little, Brown & Company, 2001.